I0499979

TACTICS TO TIME MANAGEMENT AND INCREASE PRODUCTIVITY.

The ultimate tool to reduce stress.

WILL GARNER

Table of contents

All rights reserved. No part
of this publication should
be reprinted or transmitted
through electronic or
mechanical printing
without permission from
the author.

Copyright © Will Garner

Chapter 1

Smart tactics to manage your time effectively.

Time management is the process of arranging and planning how to split your time across various tasks. Do it correctly, and you'll wind up working smarter, not harder, to get more done in less time even when time is short and demands are high. The top performers manage their time extraordinarily effectively.

Here's how to get started:

1. Know how you're spending your time

If your productivity is judged by production over a given timeframe, missed time might mean cash out the window. Much like making a budget, you have to monitor what you're spending your time on to identify any areas or behaviors that are keeping you from accomplishing your objectives.

Start with a time check. Time-tracking programs like Rescue time can tell you, according to the categories you put up, how many hours you're productive in a day vs how much time you're spending on non-work-related activities, such as surfing social media or shopping.

2. Adhere to a regular program

Go beyond "I have eight hours to complete XYZ." Set a daily plan with appropriate time blocks for various chores. Sticking to it is the key to success.

Build realistic timeframes. Humans overestimate their potential to get things done, a condition scientists term "planning fallacy," which frequently results in excessively optimistic delivery forecasts. Create time buffers between activities so that even if one goes beyond the time restriction, the entire schedule remains consistent. Remember, self-discipline is your greatest friend here.

3. Prioritise

To-do lists may be productivity lifesavers. Yet if you're not cautious, they might grow so enormous and overpowering that you don't know where to start. A technique called the Eisenhower Matrix may help you select what to prioritise according to priority and urgency. With this choice matrix, you may break down your list by:

Do immediately: Critical activities with set dates, or ones you've put off for so long they're already late
Timetable for later: Critical activities with no specified timeframes
Delegate: Things that someone else can accomplish
Delete Activities you can remove since they're not vital to your aims or purpose

4. Do the most difficult assignment first

Distractions happen to all of us, whether it's a phone call, a favour from a colleague, or that pile of dirty dishes. Next thing you know, the day is gone. It's time to "eat that frog."

The Eat That Frog productivity method devised by leadership expert Brian Tracy works well for people who tend to procrastinate or have trouble avoiding distractions. It recommends tackling the biggest, most difficult, and most important task first—the one you're likely to put off for later. Only move on to other things once you've "eaten that frog."

5. Batch-process similar tasks

Batching, or batch processing means grouping similar tasks so you can work on them together. Group them by objective or function. For example:

Client meetings on Wednesdays and Thursdays
Respond to emails from 10 to 11 a.m. only
Generate reports first thing in the morning, and distribute them.

6. Set reasonable time limits

Parkinson's law states that "Work expands to fill the time allotted to complete it."
If you have a full day to complete two tasks that should take only three hours, you'll probably still spend the whole day on those two tasks. If you give yourself a smaller window, chances are you'll still meet the earlier deadline.

7. Learn when to say no

We have only so much energy in a day, and it wanes with the hours. To avoid half-baked work, know your limits and be willing to say no. Recognize your strengths and weaknesses. Focus on what you're good at and, if possible, delegate what can be done better and faster by other people.

8. Avoid multitasking

The science is clear on multitasking: It cuts efficiency and can even be dangerous. According to the American Psychological Association, mental juggling involves "switching costs" that slash productivity. Although task switching might cost only a few seconds per switch, it adds up if you multitask frequently. Your risk for error also soars.

Why is time management important in a team?

First, we should briefly overview how proper team time management helps the overall workflow and inter-team relations.

Time management reduces stress.

Time management is not only crucial to getting things done on time, but it can also decrease the risk of potential health issues. Experts from the Stress Management Society have often warned that poor time management leads to stress. And it's not just about missed deadlines or staying overtime.

When people have trouble managing their time or find it difficult to prioritise their tasks, they inevitably end up feeling overwhelmed.

Being overwhelmed further causes people to be:

Nervous, Afraid of missing important information or tasks, Misreading situations, and so much more.

The brain can then get stuck into panic mode in which case, the person who responds to the stressful situation makes mistakes or completely collapses under pressure.

And within a team, different people will react differently to stress caused by poor time management. This situation can further cause inter-team conflict as person A can accuse person B of being too relaxed, or person B can accuse person A of being too nervous.

So, good time management on a team level can then significantly improve team dynamics and alleviate some of the work stress they face daily.

Time management ensures everyone remains updated.

Transparency never went out of style. However, even with all the apps and services designed to help us keep track of what everyone does at any moment, we're still mostly in the dark when it comes to our coworkers' part of the job. Still, communication concerning task progress is vital for the health of a team and the project itself.

But, with improved team time management skills, transparency increases. Prioritizing becomes easier when everyone is tracking what they're working on and they're aware of everything that's on their co-worker's plates. There's even less prodding and poking on the group chat to report on progress and certainly fewer meetings.

Once the team starts to track their time collectively, you can start to see the bigger picture more clearly as time goes by. It becomes easier to follow the project's progress, and in addition, eliminates the need to ask how everything is going. It is much easier to create reports and hold meetings.

Team members will begin getting an idea of how their time management reflects on the overall project. Their coworkers will also be able to see that and address any problems in due time.

Time management increases project transparency.

Transparency is important when managing projects because it makes the team work harder and better. It shows how well a project is performing, builds trust among team members, and keeps work on track.

When the entire team knows their goals and their specific roles, they will function more effectively as a whole.

One way to improve project transparency is to practise proper time management habits that will help you take your project management system to a different level. Effective time management is key to the project's success, and without it, the team will be left confused and disorganised.

To improve project transparency by introducing time-tracking software, which will also accelerate project progress. Once the team starts to track their time collectively, you can start to see the bigger picture more clearly as time goes by.

Time tracking makes it easier to:

- Follow the project progress,

Create reports and hold meetings, and Eliminate the need to ask how everything is going.
As soon as they start tracking their time, team members will get an idea of how their time management reflects on the overall project, and address problems in due time.

Furthermore, try to be open with your team about your projects and processes, and create a system where all team members will have easy access to relevant information. Team members are more likely to support each other when they understand what everyone is doing as a whole.

Time management improves collaboration.

People are more inclined to help each other when they're in the same proverbial boat. When a team tracks their time and learns how to manage it together, they will be more likely to help each other out when mistakes happen.

Chapter 2

The power of making proper priorities and strategies.

Throughout the workday, duties are frequently prioritised or not depending on the requirements of others or the urgency of deadlines. This may happen in our personal life, too, with minimal time spent on genuinely essential tasks, and more energy spent being "busy." Prioritising activities successfully with purpose and according to future objectives may alter this, ensuring that every work you perform creates value and prevents trivial chores from cluttering your to-do list.

By applying prioritising tactics, you may significantly modify the arc of your workday to make the most of your time in the workplace and at home. Whether you're a lone entrepreneur or an executive, these tactics can help you analyse and define your top goals.

ways for prioritising activities at work.

Effective prioritising often entails setting an agenda, analysing activities, and allocating time and labour to offer the maximum value in a short time.

1. Have a list that comprises all tasks

Good prioritising comes from recognizing the whole breadth of what you need to get done even the most routine activities should be written down and examined. To offer yourself a comprehensive view, it's a good idea to combine both personal and working chores in a single task list.

Everything from picking up your dry cleaning to organising a one-on-one meeting with your supervisor should be logged in the same location. After everything is written down, prioritising normally occurs according to the significance, urgency, duration, and reward of each activity.

Determine what's important: Knowing your actual aims.

Although it could appear like an urgent time management method, prioritising is crucial in accomplishing long-term objectives. Knowing what you're working toward—be it a promotion, a completed project, or a career change—helps you select the activities most essential to those future outcomes. It might be a good idea to split these bigger objectives into smaller, time-related ones. For example, an annual objective may be deconstructed into monthly to-do lists, which subsequently lead to weekly chores, daily priorities, etc.

2: Determine what's important: Knowing your genuine aims.

Although it could appear like an urgent time management method, prioritising is crucial in accomplishing long-term objectives. Knowing what you're working toward—be it a promotion, a completed project, or a career change—helps you select the activities most essential to those future outcomes. It might be a good idea to split these bigger objectives into smaller, time-related ones. For example, an annual objective may be deconstructed into monthly to-do lists, which subsequently lead to weekly chores, daily priorities, etc.

3. Evaluate the worth of your tasks.

Take a look at your key job and evaluate what provides the most value to your company and organisation. As a general rule, you want to understand precisely which sorts of jobs are vital and have top priority over the rest.

For example, concentrate on client projects before internal work; putting up the new CEO's computer before re-configuring the database; responding to support tickets before developing training materials, and so on. Another method to determine value is to look at how many individuals are influenced by your work. In general, the more individuals engaged or affected, the greater the stakes.

Following are some useful resources to estimate the worth and relevance of your job.

- Urgent priorities are time-sensitive and of high value. They include responsibilities coping with emergencies or stringent customer deadlines.
- High-value projects that are not time urgent should be regarded as a high priority. These are jobs that need to be thought of, planned, and teamwork.
- Middle priority might be time urgent but not high in value. Meetings, email exchanges, and project organising might fall within this category.

- Low-priority projects and tasks are not time urgent and do not have great value. You may postpone these objectives until later in the week or drop them completely.

4. Sort tasks by estimated effort.

If you have projects that appear to tie for priority standing, examine their estimates, and start on whichever one you believe will require the greatest work to finish. Productivity gurus advocate the approach of beginning the longer activity first. Yet, if you feel like you can't concentrate on your meatier assignments until you completely off the shorter work, then go with your gut and accomplish that. It might be motivational to tick a little item off the list before plunging into deeper seas.

Handling uncertainty is hard work. If you're seeking additional information on establishing accurate project estimates, check out how LiquidPlanner leverages Smart Estimation via our project management product, Planning Intelligence.

5. Be flexible and adaptive.

Uncertainty and change are given. Recognize that your priorities will change, and frequently when you least expect them to. So prepare for the unexpected. But—and here's the trick—you also want to keep focused on the things you're committed to completing. When working on such activities, strive to foresee additional project needs that will follow your priority so you may better prepare for what is ahead.

Chapter 3

Design a structure that keeps distractions .

Whether you're working from home, in your favourite coffee shop, or in a bustling office, distractions have become a familiar fixture of the modern workplace. In some cases, specifically for creative tasks, distractions can be a good thing. That may sound counterintuitive but distractions can help us get out of a rut known as cognitive fixation. We also have an internal urge to be distracted.

However, considering that we get interrupted every 11 minutes and it takes 25 minutes for our brains to refocus on the original task -- workplace distractions should be avoided as much as possible.

According to a survey conducted by Udemy, workplace distractions negatively impact performance, productivity, and potential. What's more, to compensate for these interruptions, people work faster. A UC Irvine study shows that this increases stress and frustration. And, even a brief interruption doubles an employee's error rate.

In short, constant distractions don't just affect the bottom line. They can also be detrimental to an individual's health.

How can you address these workplace distractions before they become an issue? You need to start by identifying what'sWhether you're working from home, your favourite coffee shop, or in a bustling office, distractions have become a familiar fixture of the modern workplace. In some cases, specifically for creative tasks, distractions can be a good thing. That may sound counterintuitive but distractions can help us get out of a rut known as cognitive fixation. We also have an internal urge to be distracted.

However, considering that we get interrupted every 11 minutes and it takes 25 minutes for our brains to refocus on the original task -- workplace distractions should be avoided as much as possible.

According to a survey conducted by Udemy, workplace distractions negatively impact performance, productivity, and potential. What's more, to compensate for these interruptions, people work faster. A UC Irvine study shows that this increases stress and frustration. And, even a brief interruption doubles an employee's error rate.

In short, constant distractions don't just affect the bottom line. They can also be detrimental to an individual's health.

How can you address these workplace distractions before they become an issue? You need to start by identifying what's exactly distracting your team. Knowing what the distraction is and how it is happening can help you make a plan to squash these interruptions.

1. Smartphones
No surprise here. After all, the average person in the U.S. views their phone 52 times a day. And, it's easy to understand why. We're

bombarded throughout the day with emails, texts, social media notifications, and phone calls. Additionally, we use our phones to jot down reminders, view our calendars, listen to a podcast, or go shopping. No wonder we're addicted.

Overcoming your reliance on your smartphone is no easy task, but it's not impossible. The tried and true methods are to put your phone on aeroplane mode or use the phone's "do not disturb" function. This action can be done on both Android or iPhone. You can also place your phone in another room or leave it in a desk drawer, bag or purse.

Scheduling specific times throughout the day also helps cut down on "during work-hours usage." For example, I turn my phone on silent when I need to focus solely on my work. Usually, this takes around two hours. After I've completed my work, I check my phone to make sure I haven't missed anything important. To ensure that I don't get too consumed, I only give myself 10 minutes of phone-time before diving back into work.

2. Emails
We send out a lot of emails. How many? Well, in 2017 a staggering 269 billion emails were sent daily worldwide. That email figure is

expected to jump to around 333 billion in 2019.

Like your smartphone, there's also the temptation to stop what you're doing and check your inbox as soon as a new message arrives. Unfortunately, if you did this all day, how could you possibly get any work done?

The easiest solution is to turn off your email notifications on your phone. You should also close any apps or web browsers containing your email. I also use an app like SaneBox to manage my inbox because it filters out the messages that aren't important.

The most important thing to remember is if there's an emergency, you aren't just going to be notified via email. People will call you or knock on your door. Everything else can wait until you have the scheduled time to go through your inbox.

3. Background noise
Take a moment and really listen to all of the noise going on in an office. People are talking, machines running, phones ringing, and doors opening/closing. That's not even getting into the annoyances like coughing, loud snacking, or music playing.

Background noise is inevitable. If it becomes too distracting, you should invest in noise-cancelling headphones or relocating to a quieter area when you need to give a task 100 percent of your attention. I've also found that apps like Noisli can drown-out background noise, while also improving my focus.

4. People interruptions
Like background noise, interruptions from employees, customers, suppliers, and family are unavoidable. Engineers on Quora identified, "shoulder tapping," as one of their most common distractions.

One way around this is keeping your office door closed when you don't want to be disturbed. For good measure, place a "do not disturb" sign on the door. If you work in an open office space, send signals like wearing headphones and being honest. If someone has a direct and work-related question, give them the answer and move on.

Another tactic is to plan for these interpretations. For example, you could block out in your calendar a period where you're available for pop-ins. I also add some buffer time between tasks and meetings. This way if someone comes to me with a question it's not going to throw my entire schedule out-of-whack.

5. Clutter

While in small doses a little clutter can encourage a creative mind, the fact is that a messy workplace affects your ability to focus and process information. Confusion and disorder are essentially a to-do-list that reminds you of everything that needs to be done. As such, it pulls you away from being present. Over time, this makes you more anxious and stressed.

The fix? Keep your workspace clean and organised. Toss out the items you no longer need. Place paperwork in the appropriate files. Ideally, you should put as much paperwork on the cloud as possible to reduce the number of filing cabinets. Make sure that all of your office supplies have a home and are returned at the end of the day.

Even if you don't do this daily, you should at least clean your workspace every week. For example, on a Friday afternoon is perfect. You've probably already mentally clocked-out for the week, so this is a soft task that can be done quickly.

6. Multi-tasking

I'm sure we've all been guilty of juggling too many tasks at once.

You're a successful entrepreneur --
why can't you juggle multiple
responsibilities at once? The truth is
that our brains are not capable of
focusing on more than one thing at a
time.

Multitasking doesn't save time or
make you more productive. It
actually slows you down. "Switching
from task to task, you think you're
actually paying attention to
everything around you at the same
time. But you're actually not,
""You're not paying attention to one
or two things simultaneously, but
switching between them very
rapidly."

Additionally, when you multitask you make more mistakes, reduce creative thinking, and are potentially damaging your brain. Multi-tasking was one of the more difficult bad habits I had to overcome. There are still times when I find myself doing more than one thing at once. I've been able to change this habit by creating blocks of time for specific tasks into my calendar app.

During this timeframe, my phone was off, and the office door closed. When my mind began to wander, I would stand-up and walk around the office for a couple of minutes to clear my head. Sounds simple, but this habit is not easy to break. Leaving my desk for a few minutes encouraged me to only focus on composing this piece instead of doing five other things at the same time. Only then did I jump into my next priority.

7. Co-workers

Conversing with your employees, colleagues, and business partners are all essential for building a friendly and collaborative company culture. However, spending too much talking about "Game of Thrones" or gossiping isn't just a major distraction. Hearsay, itself, can also create a toxic workplace.

As a leader, you just can not allow gossip in the workplace. It needs to be addressed and handled immediately -- even if it's something dire like letting an employee go. As for friendly chit-chat, you need to set boundaries.

If someone engages you in a conversation, and you're busy, politely tell them that you currently don't have time to talk, but you can catch-up during lunch. And, as mentioned above, you can also send-out signals without saying anything by wearing headphones when you don't want to be disturbed.

1. Smartphones
No surprise here. After all, the average person in the U.S. views their

phone 52 times a day. And, it's easy to understand why. We're bombarded throughout the day with emails, texts, social media notifications, and phone calls. Additionally, we use our phones to jot down reminders, view our calendars, listen to a podcast, or go shopping. No wonder we're addicted.

Overcoming your reliance on your smartphone is no easy task, but it's not impossible. The tried and true methods are to put your phone on airplane mode or use the phone's "do not disturb" function. This action can be done on both Android and iPhone. You can also place your phone in another room or leave it in a desk drawer, bag, or purse.

Scheduling specific times throughout the day also helps cut down on "during work-hours usage." For example, I turn my phone on silent when I need to focus solely on my work. Usually, this takes around two hours. After I've completed my work, I check my phone to make sure I haven't missed anything important. To ensure that I don't get too consumed, I only give myself 10 minutes of phone time before diving back into work.

2. Emails

We send out a lot of emails. How many? Well, in 2017 a staggering 269 billion emails were sent daily worldwide. That email figure is expected to jump to around 333 billion in 2019.

Like your smartphone, there's also the temptation to stop what you're doing and check your inbox as soon as a new message arrives. Unfortunately, if you did this all day, how could you possibly get any work done?

The easiest solution is to turn off your email notifications on your phone. You should also close any apps or web browsers containing your email. I also use an app like SaneBox to manage my inbox because it filters out the messages that aren't important.

The most important thing to remember is if there's an emergency, you aren't just going to be notified via email. People will call you or knock on your door. Everything else can wait until you have the scheduled time to go through your inbox.

3. Background noise
Take a moment and listen to all of the noise going on in an office. People are talking, machines running, phones ringing, and doors opening/closing. That's not even getting into the annoyances like coughing, loud snacking, or music playing.

Background noise is inevitable. If it becomes too distracting, you should invest in noise-cancelling headphones or relocate to a quieter area when you need to give a task 100 percent of your attention. I've also found that apps like Noisli can drown-out background noise, while also improving my focus.

4. People interruptions
Like background noise, interruptions from employees, customers, suppliers, and family are unavoidable. Engineers on Quora identified, "shoulder tapping," as one of their most common distractions.

One way around this is keeping your office door closed when you don't want to be disturbed. For good measure, place a "do not disturb" sign on the door. If you work in an open office space, send signals like wearing headphones and being honest. If someone has a direct and work-related question, give them the answer and move on.

Another tactic is to plan for these interpretations. For example, you could block out in your calendar a period when you're available for pop-ins. I also add some buffer time between tasks and meetings. This way if someone comes to me with a question it's not going to throw my entire schedule out of whack.

5. Clutter

While in small doses a little clutter can encourage a creative mind, the fact is that a messy workplace affects your ability to focus and process information. Confusion and disorder are essentially a to-do list that reminds you of everything that needs to be done. As such, it pulls you away from being present. Over time, this makes you more anxious and stressed.

The fix? Keep your workspace clean and organized. Toss out the items you no longer need. Place paperwork in the appropriate files. Ideally, you should put as much paperwork on the cloud as possible to reduce the number of filing cabinets. Make sure that all of your office supplies have a home and are returned at the end of the day.

Even if you don't do this daily, you should at least clean your workspace every week. For example, a Friday afternoon is perfect. You've probably already mentally clocked out for the week, so this is a soft task that can be done quickly.

6. Multi-tasking

I'm sure we've all been guilty of juggling too many tasks at once.

You're a successful entrepreneur --
why can't you juggle multiple
responsibilities at once? The truth is
that our brains are not capable of
focusing on more than one thing at a
time.

Multitasking doesn't save time or
make you more productive. It slows
you down. "Switching from task to
task, you think you're paying
attention to everything around you
at the same time. But you're not,
"You're not paying attention to one
or two things simultaneously, but
switching between them very
rapidly."

Additionally, when you multitask
you make more mistakes, reduce

creative thinking, and are potentially damaging your brain. Multi-tasking was one of the more difficult bad habits I had to overcome. There are still times when I find myself doing more than one thing at once. I've been able to change this habit by creating blocks of time for specific tasks in my calendar app.

During this timeframe, my phone was off, and the office door closed. When my mind began to wander, I would stand up and walk around the office for a couple of minutes to clear my head. Sounds simple, but this habit is not easy to break. Leaving my desk for a few minutes encouraged me to only focus on composing this piece instead of doing five other things at the same time. Only then did I jump into my next priority?

7. Co-workers

Conversing with your employees, colleagues, and business partners is essential for building a friendly and collaborative company culture. However, spending too much talking about "Game of Thrones" or gossiping isn't just a major distraction. Hearsay, itself, can also create a toxic workplace.

As a leader, you just can not allow gossip in the workplace. It needs to be addressed and handled immediately -- even if it's something dire like letting an employee go. As for friendly chit-chat, you need to set boundaries.

If someone engages you in a conversation, and you're busy, politely tell them that you currently don't have time to talk, but you can catch up with them during lunch. And, as mentioned above, you can also send out signals without saying anything by wearing headphones when you don't want to be disturbed.

Chapter 4

Create a productive daily routine.

Figuring out how to create a daily routine that works for you and how to stick to it can take some time. What should your perfect daily routine contain? That depends on your needs. Figure out what you have to get done and when. You also need to be honest about your lifestyle, including your bandwidth and time-management abilities, to create a reasonable work routine you can stick to.

Here are five steps to help you make a daily routine for yourself, even if you've never had one.

Make a List
Figuring out how to write a daily routine begins by writing down everything you need to get done daily, both at home and at work. Don't worry about how you organise this list; this is a brain dump, not a to-do list. Simply jot down everything you do each day, as well as everything you should get done.

If you feel like it's too hard to remember all the tasks in one sitting, carry around a notebook to take notes throughout the day. No task is too small if you want to work "brush teeth" into your daily routine, put it on the list.

Structure Your Day
Early birds tend to get things done most effectively before lunchtime while night owls get their burst of energy in the evenings. Think about when you work best. Then, group your tasks into the time of day that makes the most sense for when you will efficiently complete them.

Mornings: Mornings are often about getting out the door, which can be its own challenge. Group all your early tasks, such as feeding and walking pets, preparing breakfast, or putting dinner in the slow cooker. For the rest of the morning, consider tasks you'll want to do while you're still fresh. Also, think about tasks that you tend to dread or procrastinate starting. Schedule them for the morning, so they're not looming over you all day.

Midday: This is a tricky time of day because your energy levels—and perhaps the caffeine from your morning coffee—have likely dissipated. This is a good time to do the boring, routine stuff that doesn't take a lot of brainpower. Use midday time for tasks like answering emails, setting appointments, and running errands. If you are based at home during the day, it's a good time to handle routine cleaning, such as emptying and loading the dishwasher or scrubbing the bathroom.

Evening: Evenings work best for planning and preparing for the next day. Lay out your clothes, pack lunches, and declutter the spaces that tend to be drop zones, such as mail piles.

Get Specific (Optional)

Get as specific as you want with your outline of tasks. For example, write a daily morning routine that looks something like this to account for time:

6:00: Wake up, shower
6:30: Breakfast, brush teeth

7:00: Leave the house
7:15: Drop off kids at school
7:30: Arrive at the office
You might prefer that level of detail—at least until you get the hang of your routine.

Schedule Time for Flexibility

The goal of creating a daily routine is to harness your most productive hours for challenging tasks and your least productive hours for mundane tasks. But life happens so prepare for unplanned events by keeping some flexible free time within your routine.

For instance, you might have a doctor's appointment during your usual work time. Or you have a social gathering at the time you typically prep the next day's lunches. Scheduling blocks of free time into your daily routine helps you shift tasks around while keeping things flowing smoothly in spite of atypical events and you'll never feel pressed for time.

www.ingramcontent.com/pod-product-compliance
Lightning Source LLC
Chambersburg PA
CBHW070459220526
45466CB00004B/1885